WELCOME! YOU ARE JUST A FEW PAGES
AWAY FROM *GROWN OCEAN*.

copyright © 2021 matt mitchell

all rights reserved. no part of this book may be used or reproduced
in any manner whatsoever without written permission from the publisher
except in the case of brief quotations in critical articles or reviews.
for more information, contact word west press.

isbn: 978-1-7369477-8-4

published by word west in brooklyn, ny.

first us edition 2021.
printed in the usa.

www.wordwest.co

cover & interior design: matt mitchell

text set in cochin

```
                            will
                 be             .
            back . am
                            with you,

                    terribly hurt
                                , but
            i'm ok now



                        love,




                    don't worry about
                    me


                        i will call
```

*an erasure of James Dean's letter to his father
before filming *Rebel Without a Cause*

GROWN OCEAN

[]

beyond the cowboys flushed in acid galloping

through the hotel parking lot, yodeling at snakes,

there's a turritopsis dohrnii in California waters.

locals call it immortal jellyfish because it reverts

to a polyp when it's stressed or sick or old.

to live inside of a reset forever, we'd only be so lucky.

I hope I can achieve the same endless do-over

and wrap my arms around your tattooed body

once I stop being an iceberg and migrate back

to the coast we left behind.

yesterday I sang into the canyons

and all that echoed back was wind.

a 76ers game on a television set in my hotel room.

they are up by 5 on the Raptors.

superstar hall of famer absolute godhead NBA center

Wilt Chamberlain slept with 20,000 women,

and if you laid all of their bodies out across the Pacific Ocean,

you would have to do it over 270 times before you could reach Asia.

behind paper thin walls, a neighboring room

is watching *Seinfeld*. we were born the spring

before the summer it ended,

the summer everyone gathered in Times Square

to watch that show about nothing.

this is a poem about nothing.

but it's also a poem about everything.

the number one song in America

was I Don't Wanna Miss a Thing

because we all knew there was so much

armageddon left to see.

my cab comes by and asks where to.

I say take me to the ocean so I can fall into it

and coo about how Japan has already started eroding

away into the shape of an Ohio we can't remember.

there is a dolphin in Italian waters.

America is selling out.

I have forgotten how to fill up a heart with familiarity.

but, if by some chance Cormac was right,

and you have my whole heart and you always did,

please, let those tides bring you home to me,

so we can relearn how to spell warmth.

so we can cut up the rug in our best chambray plumes,

dance, and glug Coca-Cola.

AirBnB ourselves a heaven on Fairfax,

dirty the sheets, and never leave, O, so help me god.

[]

on a 6 AM plane

coming to Ohio from Texas

when you were hungover and the

cabin lights buzzed your eyes shut

You fell asleep on my shoulder

right after takeoff and stayed

that way the whole flight

Such an insignificant thing to hold onto

but what a gift it was to finally

have a body small but trusted

At least enough for you to sleep

against it in a vacuum-sealed room

of chairs that could've fallen

from the sky at any moment

I did not know I would marry you

when the stewardess brought us 2 Cokes

I drank them both real quick

I was so worried the rattling of the glass

on your tray table would wake you

[]

I started loving you

long before my prefrontal cortex was fully-developed,

before I made you my emergency contact,

when we both jackknifed into the college pool,

and you said mine was a 10 and I said yours was a 9,

because you knew how to swim and I didn't.

when we cannonballed consecutively

and made splashes so big they excavated the whole campus,

and we had to make a break for it.

then 2 years later we solved the Cleveland Torso Murders

together, which felt really out of the blue and unlike us,

because it had already been a cold case for 70 years,

and we were never all that good at taking care of cold things,

especially our bodies in winter,

when the apartment heater would kick off before dawn.

but on some Wednesday evening,

you put your hand into the hole of my thigh,

where the lip of a needle once gripped,

and pulled out a sky empty of airplanes,

when truthfully I expected you to pull out nothing,

except maybe a rotten fruit or burnt atoms

or cilantro that tastes like soap.

I admit I have always been a sissy,

that I only ever bring knives to gunfights.

all of that and you still stay.

you could run like an egg, but you stay.

[]

After 3 consecutive episodes, Netflix asks me

if Jason Bateman and I are still enjoying the coo

of this specific heaven—where we are nothing

but paid-off mortgages floating around cars

in rush hour traffic. I say yes and pull Jason Bateman in real close

just so I can study his perfectly-symmetrical face.

We chew the juice out of our after dinner gum and spit at the earth.

I ask him what he plans to do with his share of the Pacific Ocean,

and he says, *turn it into a zoo for endangered glaciers*.

He pauses. *Or just give it all away*, he adds.

We selfie by a city once a vacant lot.

I Instagram it and tag the moon.

I make a hashtag out of his jawline,

and it becomes the first hashtag that can cut glass.

He calls me a beach and leaves a good Yelp review about my collarbones.

He says he has really been getting into Buddy Holly lately

When Jason Bateman and I kiss,

the 5th dentist caves and recommends Trident gum.

He kisses with his eyes closed, like god intended.

Jason Bateman's mouth tastes like the inside of a lava lamp. Electric.

We climb mountains to break hearts. We eat birds to become birds.

We take a dip together in the nearby lake

just to see who can hold their breath underwater longer.

Below the surface, I cheat and say *I love you*.

We come up for air. He asks, *Did you say something?*

and I say, *I asked 'How are you'*.

[]

you are the one who taught me that giraffes

were once made of trees.

that they were gorgeous like backyard birds.

that birds are dinosaurs,

which means giraffes are prettier than dinosaurs.

I wonder if the dinosaurs saw the asteroid

and thought here come the stars.

look, they're coming home.

I wonder if the cosmonauts piloting the asteroid

saw the dinosaurs and thought

look at all of those beautiful giraffes.

o, god, they must be made of trees.

[]

On our first date, we rented a kitchen from IKEA. And by rented, I mean we just sort of saw the display and called it ours for the night. It came with a table, so we thrifted some blankets and pillows from a bedroom display. *watch this*, you said. So, of course I did. I watched you throw the blankets high in the air and I watched them float down, beautifully, like microfiber parachutes, and land perfectly on top of the table. We lined the pillows around each side of the table until they became a fortress. I brought glow-in-the-dark sticky stars and stuck them to the underbelly of the table. Everything was yellow. We played songs on my phone, but I kept rewinding the chorus of Never My Love by The Association, so I guess we really only played one song. But it was our song. You told me you were first obsessed with palindromes. But then you were really obsessed with D.B. Cooper, especially obsessed with how he jumped from a moving plane and lost his shoe mid-plummet and said *it happens to everybody* before disappearing. On a piece of printer paper you lifted from the back room while the store manager showcased a refrigerator, you wrote NO ENTRY in black sharpie. And you taped it onto a doorway we made out of backpacks. And when the store manager finally found us, of course he wanted in. Who wouldn't. But he couldn't guess the password, so we laughed and giggled and kissed while he rattled off a thousand incorrect words, never knowing the password was just 1-2-3-4. It was right then and there when I found the river in god's mouth. Right then and there when I couldn't wait to buy you a city and make it an ocean. Couldn't imagine doing anything else but spending our whole lives hiding in that blanket fort, just waiting for the other shoe to drop. and another and another and another.

[]

the freezing rain falling on the air conditioner

sounds like a butterfly of soda fluttering in its can

while we watch *Funny People* again.

cigarette smell gets caught in the doorstop,

cars honk beneath the cleft of our living room window.

deer jaywalking across 4-lane traffic again, I'll bet.

hey pause it, will you? I have to pee

and quickly retweet that published poem

I posted about 10 hours ago, again, for more heart clicks.

hey don't forget to email the weather and ask

if we're cooking at home or eating out tomorrow night.

I love you, too. yes, I promise. pinky swear.

okay you can hit play.

there goes the salt truck again. heading north this time.

the winters here are always so beautiful, aren't they.

I imagine we could just walk outside,

catch snow on our tongues, slip on the slick

of a wet step, and fall into a hug of earth glowingly.

no, I'm not sobbing

because of the Wilco song on the soundtrack.

yes, I know that would be completely on brand for me.

it's actually because of Adam Sandler's character,

how he fears the universe is growing without him

and that he's lost his shot at the whole *our love is all we have* thing.

it's a totally reasonable and completely relatable fear.

no, I'm not going to metaphor that into a poem, I promise.

dammit, Apple News says Jupiter got another moon.

do you want to get married tomorrow?

[]

they say god created the earth in seven days.

and then, on the eighth day,

he created Wawa convenience stores.

but then, George Harrison wrote a song

titled Wah-Wah. but that was so long ago

I'm not even sure who was first anymore.

it's kind of a chicken and egg deal for me, personally.

my high school biology teacher

liked to dissect animals with us

and pull their carcasses apart like rotisserie chicken,

just to put them back together at the end of class.

he taught us about evolution,

how there was the made-from-scratch bacteria

and the acid washed jeans. then the bath salt zombies

and the aurora borealis,

but before it was aurora borealis,

when we only knew it as sky,

when daylight savings time

was just early morning coupon cutting.

if the ice age had abided by daylight savings time,

maybe there'd have been no melt.

maybe there's a tear in the space-time-continuum

we can climb through to go back

and flex-seal the Titanic.

of course there's the risk of endangering

the icebergs. it's a big what if.

but what if The Strokes had never left New York City.

what if the Jazz had beaten the Bulls in seven.

what if our bodies are bursting,

just waiting to be put back together.

[]

before bed, I put your ears on the shelf,

inside a plastic container, next to the buffalo nickels.

rolled on your side, you ask, *which mouth*

will carry us into morning this time,

while a muted Netflix glows into our ceiling,

and we dream of the old world,

where god used USPS 2-day priority shipping

to mail the chicken cross-pangaea,

and then the whole-shelled egg came sometime after.

there was the asteroid and kids old as the cascades,

and the bottle-necked shore so full of undiscovered fish

we ate ourselves into a new species.

our mitochondria, beholdenly glacial and ugly,

already stuffed with laughlight hyacinth,

gap-tooth doorway dark,

and hands book-pressed into leaves.

but it's the new world, and Sisyphus is pushing

and pushing and pushing our love over the border line,

over the equator of fleeting Middle American

spaghetti-strap tan, until it collapses down.

we are nothing without the ocean, which has grown

wider than an arm's length and yellowed accordingly.

our throats gone platinum like 1984 hairdressings.

our throats longing for the days

when we read all the poetry together.

the earth honeyed with laughter,

collectively I am nothing

but sharp hip bones, reused cells, and AndroGel.

half-asleep, you roll over and lift my shirt

and find nothing but snow.

the neighbors above us are cutting up the rug

while the crosswalk pigeons siren pedestrians along outside.

we kiss, as is custom, and tell each other goodnight.

you turn back over, pull my arm across your body,

and say, *I don't want you to go. not yet.*

darling, we lost our whole yard to city construction

and sold our bicycles for bottled lightning.

how could I possibly leave you now,

when there are stars still pregnant with us,

carrying our cosmic, dumb little bodies to term.

[]

the problem with sunsets is they are infinitesimal and consecutive. and our bodies live in cars forever speeding to catch them. how ridiculous, to fear there will not be another one tomorrow. the problem is fish-hook mouth and mesozoic extinction. Nickelodeon reboot fantastical and classroom holiday party exclusion singularities. we are always running and running. to where? a bedroom where summer nights come alive and our bodies are nothing but overdue library books. we are constantly sticking our hot fingers in glasses of Coke and poking at the ice cubes. because it was us who demanded the melt. but who cooks the cookbooks after the recipes are all used? I have never roomed with a sky that didn't talk back when I asked about rain. never met a person who thinks the Temptations got better when David Ruffin left. I can't remember the last time I stopped talking and appreciated the way footsteps echo. where Northern Oregon and Southern Washington kiss, I took a picture of erosion and figured it used to be something. maybe once an iceberg, I captioned on Instagram. when we first moved in together, we both brought our film collections and learned we have duplicate copies of *Stand By Me* on DVD. and it occurred to me last night, when we were both standing face to face on each side of our bedroom doorway, as the window behind you dressed your back in sunlight, and the light of our living room television glowed against mine, that we hadn't looked at each other from that close of a proximity in ages. moments like those, they make you wish your life was always so parallel. I am sorry to announce I am terrified I will fall in love with the next pair of pants cut into shorts I see. afraid even the Vine compilations will leave us, too. when NASA mentioned an alternate universe evolving in reverse, everyone became an ocean itching for California to fall into them. eons ago mermaids lived with the dinosaurs, until the executive continental drift committee heard a disturbance on Earth. so they decided to go investigate. and when the dinosaurs stopped barking, they say there finally came rain.

[]

I am on the phone with you

while watching *The Last Waltz* on a television

in a different state. you ask me what's going on,

so I tell you Neil is here and he is singing so hard

he budges the coke rock from the clutches of his nose canal.

and there is Joni, because how could there not be Joni,

and she is singing background vocals

better than Neil is singing lead vocals,

but she is singing behind the stage's curtain,

for mysterious effect,

so I guess we're not supposed to know it's her.

but we all know it's her. we always know.

I tell you Neil's harmonica is, realistically,

probably made of wood or injection-molded plastic,

but I think we should just be hyperbolic

and say it is actually made of butterflies.

there is Rick Danko being cute like always,

and there is Robbie Robertson smirking

his electric 10 dollar asshole smirk.

but I can't see Levon Helm, I'm sorry, I say.

I know he is your favorite.

you ask what else,

so I tell you there are the yellow moons

and the blue, blue windows and the stars

and the babes singing with me somehow.

there is the San Francisco ocean really watching

its hugging shore for the first time,

finally realizing, *My god this is so beautiful.*

I could put it on top of the junk chair

across the room and look at it forever.

[]

you won a John Glenn science award in high school.

to be called an astronaut without touching

space, that must be both beautiful and devastating.

you told me I could go to the moon if I want,

even if I've never won a John Glenn science award.

when I was 6, I wanted to be a professional basketball player.

I'm 23 now, and I still don't know how to be that.

I once fell in love with my art teacher, who had a tattoo

of Honey Boo-Boo's mom on his right thigh.

when someone drew a dick in permanent marker

on the geometry teacher's floor,

the art teacher said

it wasn't Matt, or else that dick would be much better drawn.

god gave us hands like lifeboats and we wasted them.

my mouth is an enemy and my brain is even worse.

the sun is 32.2 billion in dog years.

imagine the shit it's done and lied about.

my therapist asks me to go on,

so I say: in 3rd grade, I dug a moat

on the playground and called it God.

and then I cursed when someone tore it apart,

banished to 10 days on the wall for saying *fuck*.

I say: in 8th grade, I quit basketball

because I shot jumpers from the chest and ran laps for it.

I say: it is my gender that killed all the buffalo

and apologized with nickels.

it is this thicket of mediocre road rage

that destroyed pangaea.

we also invented Coke Zero.

how could you love any of this.

nobody should.

it's all incomplete, scrapped, and restarted.

there's a strip of Highway 30 in Iowa that looks like Ohio,

with its farming malls and agricultural spaceships.

there's me and I'm reading Bromfield

in my mother's car on our way west,

still thinking about games of smear the queer

in backyards and on lunchroom linoleum

10 years after the fact.

thinking of the ways we called each other faggots

but in a totally straight way

by the lunar module dedicated to Neil Armstrong,

next to a McDonald's that never cleaned its soda fountains,

next to a Super K-Mart's corpse

and a graveyard of butterflies.

everybody is always giving us

the benefit of the doubt,

even the highway of deer carcass stink

and rumble strip DayQuil.

the son who murdered his mother on the county line

and the man who abandoned the golf course

now overgrown with ragweed and lemongrass.

we could've stopped them, couldn't we?

and what about us at the party,

leaning into each other by the fire pit,

saying we'll kiss boys someday.

how naive of us, to think we could just leave

all of it behind and deserve to.

how bullshit of me, to take responsibility

for a cock that wasn't mine.

my therapist says I am missing the point,

that we all just want to be loved and touched

by a sky unaware of all the ways

we have been left undone.

c'mon, she says, let's go see it.

while we've still got some light.

[]

us: fucking underneath the weight of an REO track

spilling out of my iPhone on the nightstand.

outside our window: a married red-winged blackbird couple

fucking in a blue pale of moonlight

before midwest extinction took them away.

across the hall: a shatter of glass and a couple's hushed yell.

remember our full bodies under blanket, behind a locked door,

sandwiched in-between two slow-dying species.

or that one post-Y2K autumn, we hung a banner

on the living room window. *Together, we will see it through* in red ink,

stitched on white cloth shaped like a pentagon.

on our porch, a red-winged blackbird had been building its nest

the entire summer in slits of the awning.

inside, you and I huddled around the coffee table,

playing Monopoly beside a *Seinfeld* rerun on the television set.

I purchased Marvin Gardens for $250;

George Costanza said the sea was angry that day.

when I think about it now, I remember there wasn't

a single bird in the entire show.

every scene of the sky as empty as anywhere else.

a blank New York cityscape immune to domestic rifts;

a singing Hudson breeze cherry-picking infinitesimal matrimony.

you're out of town now and the couple across the hall

are outside yelling against the cement stairs.

I can hear them from our bed. outside, High Street like a belt

enveloping our apartment, traffic glides through quietly,

save for the dull murmur of 95.3 WZLR, "The Eagle,"

crawling out of Chevrolet dashboards.

everyone else is hidden behind chain-locked doors

and the sky is full of birds. every Ohio species is swarming

above their coughing heads, except for the red-winged blackbirds.

because all the other birds remember to warn us

of our own stupid oblivions, knowing all too well

who the sky chooses to swallow and who to abandon.

[]

tell me how all of my high school crushes are getting married.

how the woman I thought I once loved in 8th grade

is about to have her first child.

if what Meat Loaf said is true,

and we're damned if we get out and damned if we don't,

let me spend the rest of my life at the Trumbull County Fair.

because I miss the big ride they rented from an amusement park in Columbus.

one so big I cannot remember its name. an ex of mine rode it once.

she told me you could palm the moon once you reached the top.

I suspect there is a big forgotten amusement park ride on every moon.

and summers are nothing but classmate weddings and half-baked reunions now.

remember when summers were fireworks in every inch of sky,

our own rain of comets. museums of color kissing hollow air.

whatever happened to sucking face by the chain-link fence

protecting the Apollo 11 replica downtown?

when we broke up with our homecoming dates in the McDonalds parking lot.

our mouths full of other mouths, teeth stained orange from discontinued Hi-C.

it is true: I don't know what the word heartbreak sounds like coming from a dying mouth,

but I do know I have never been brave enough to go on an amusement park ride.

I have never been brave enough to touch the stars. maybe I could have married them.

☐

worshipping satan and touching each other's butts by the Coke cooler

in a Sunoco near the airfield, do you remember

when you played the song from *Big* on an out of tune dorm basement piano,

while killer clowns chased freshmen through the college streets? I hope so.

scary to think we have been together since the iPhone 8.

cool to know you will someday be Princess Diana's 10th cousin by marriage.

so let's eat the hot dogs off the roller-grill like they're buckets of royal oysters,

while our cars tongue the flooding outside. pay off the blue slushies

and scratchers in 2-dollar bills. look, a happy cartoon tree on a thinking of you card

made from a dead tree for the fam up north. *how many dead bodies*

have been planted into trees or pressed into vinyl records,

we ask each other at the same time. jinx, I hide a Coke for you

inside the lining of my jacket. I'll stop the world and melt with you,

the store ceiling sings. a blob of testosterone put a stain beneath the pocket of my skinny jeans cut lopsidedly at the kneecap.

my 16th great grandfather rode in on the Mayflower, for god's sake,

and now there are those wispy jetstreams above as if flowers stretching themselves thin

in sunlight. titanium hips from cremated bodies sometimes become airplane parts.

the big rig driver talks parking lot swelling with rainwater blues,

how electric to afford being both big and small, to be worried about the water,

when there's a birthmark on my hip shaped like a lake. back home,

in my bathtub, those tiny dinosaurs that grow in water aren't so tiny anymore.

the compostable SunChip bags I buried at age twelve just don't wanna decompose.

we've seen the world and it's getting better all the time!

there are small bits of burnt bodies above us in the sky as I write this.

they are almost gone. oh god how on earth can we let them,

[]

we went to a screening of *The Shining*

at the Cedar Lee in the Heights one summer.

it was an afternoon showing, a 3 o'clock getaway,

because matinees fuck and that's on god.

we each got Coke and popcorn and milk duds.

we stuck our faces up close

to the neon of the coming soon posters.

we played the pre-movie trivia because it's tradition.

you didn't know any of the answers because it's tradition.

the lights dimmed and the previews each said a prayer

before saying goodnight to all six of us in the theater.

glow-bellied and loose-leaf electric cerebral,

a movie theater sun looks good on you.

there was the opening shot, the shot we've seen a million times.

the autumn leaves and the western vacancy of untouched land.

T H E   S H I N I N G   in Microsoft Word default font,

its powder blue serif body forever nothing but water.

we giggled at the beauty of such a misleading introduction

and started making out quietly, but brightly,

because our bodies were so much more than water.

they were ecosmart light bulbs wearing denim jackets,

or two potato clocks dainty, pearled, and tonguing rainbow.

they say as soon as you set a clock it already starts going slow,

which must explain why we were making out.

our meridian lips afraid of losing time,

that guy four rows back yelled at us,

asking how could we possibly be making out during this.

and I said to him, *How could you not be making out during this?*

[]

Del Sol Kung Fu and Yoga became a bird sanctuary

before the pandemic. but now everyone has forgotten

about ornithology because there are no more birds.

just microchipped government feather drones

and AI robot nuclear warhead

Terminator 2: Judgement Day bees.

I have never been stung by a real bee, knock on wood.

no cankered rodeo of swollen body

turning jelly red under YMCA pool chlorine.

I almost drowned there.

can you imagine if grime-tiled tidal waves had been

the death of all men. we'd only be so lucky,

to have all hedonistic swelts of Fortnite rage eradicated

before ever earning a beginning.

there was a time when Del Sol was still kung fu and yoga.

back when I didn't miss chasing armadillo electric

in blue Austin night. hill country wasn't so steep

when we were galloping behind good carbon.

when we were two sets of running legs

and a couple of chests buzzing with estrogen.

I love you, I text from a Long Beach motel.

there's a television full of glowing hollow bodies

running suicides into the sunset, *tell me about the thinness*

of California fireflies, you reply

while you wait at the Kyoto train station.

we used to go everywhere together, and now we can't

go anywhere. the glowing ampersand by

the old Isleys building is burnt out.

Heart the band is now more Google-searched

than heart the organ,

but after quarantine we will go outside

in honor of maskless skinny dipping rendezvous

and kissing each other on our glistening foreheads

again. our app-store birth charts will feel alive,

when we are c-section suns,

stimulus check moons,

Adam Sandler movie marathon rising.

and of course I will go outside,

because I am obsessed with celebrations

dedicated to things that have gone but will return.

honeybean, binary star, lighthouse made of a thousand hands:

I splash sign language into the Pacific Ocean beneath you.

we're gonna become birds one day, I text back,

praying you catch the last shinkansen before dusk.

[]

I cannot sleep until I listen to

Radio Ga Ga by Queen 23 times in a row

Yes, absolutely, the world is going to end.

Why?

because there's a whole part of Maryland

named Chevy Chase

and no part of Maryland

named Gilda Radner.

because the aluminum shortage killed Vanilla Coke.

and because there is no god.

if there was a god,

we'd still have the Seattle Supersonics.

me at four years old, thinking

I made all the puddles go extinct

by stomping through them.

me at four years old, mistaking

drought for death.

My great aunt once dated a guy

who played pro ball for Cleveland.

maybe they were just friends,

but in my mind they loved each other.

she sat at his bedside when he was sick.

when will they run out

of phone numbers?

my bucket list is nothing

but visiting that place in America

where you can touch 4 states at one time.

Uncle Ben's death on *Ozark*

hollowed me into an exit sign,

but I blamed it on this town.

I hope the world does end,

because, then, there'll be nothing left

but buckeye groves.

because, then, when this is over,

we're all going to have to answer

to the Coca-Cola company.

because I'd sit alone,

and watch your light.

[]

after spending the whole summer inside,

we hike a block away from our apartment

to see the local high school football team play

their homecoming game on the first day of autumn.

we pay no attention to the zoo fugitive giraffe

hiding behind the Jeni's, or the 10-car build-up

on the Olentangy River up there.

all we care about is the linemen

brains going through osmosis

at the bottom of the dogpile

near midfield before halftime.

we don't know the names of any of these kids

concussing each other into wall trophies

underneath high-beamed stadium lights,

but it's so nice to turn our voices on again

and remember what they used to sound like.

[]

everyone's favorite celebrities keep dying

but you are still here, so therefore I am okay

what could be more beautiful than a Tuesday evening

NY strip steak my own hands can barely cut,

when every hidden inch of me will soon be a bruise,

and whatever I am only exists when renewed

on Wednesday nights, by a tip of pinprick touching

exhausted fat, under glow of living room light,

as I reintroduce my fingers to my thighs weekly

yes we look like fools sitting on the same side of a booth

at this Outback Steakhouse, trying to talk to each other

over movie soundtrack radio, but I need you close,

close enough to at least dig the pads of your fingers

into my shoulder blades, if the withdrawal kicks in early,

especially if we start telling the waitress our orders

in Australian accents and I just can't get through it all

▢

you, suturing your swimming body

to the horizon. a skin like sleeves of salt

turned orange candy by new morning.

your smallness cauterizing what open gap

is left in the ocean's teeth, clawing your toes

against a floor of bull kelp carcasses

and coral lifeboats cracked down the belly.

I sleep on your pillow while you're away

and let my body become the smell

you left behind. rain taps at the window:

sounds like our future kid breathing

beneath your chest. like cardinals clipping

every edge of telephone wire. but then again

there's you, buoying somewhere under

a marigold of Carolina sun, holding your hands

up to the sky, each finger cracking

like a grandfather clock. you say I love you

to an ending you can't see,

but all I hear is the water. I need you

so much closer. so come on. come on.

[]

there's a scene in the *Evil Genius* documentary on Netflix

where Bill Rothstein calls the cops about a dead body hidden in his icebox.

but, as I'm watching this all play out,

with you and your curiosity,

washing my dinner of chicken nuggets down with a root beer,

I can only think about that William Carlos Williams poem you showed me,

the one about the plums in his icebox and his subsequent consumption of them.

instead of immersing myself in the complicated plot

of the Erie Pizza Bomber bank heist,

I like imagining Bill Rothstein on the phone with the Erie Police,

admitting to keeping a grandiose arrangement of plums in his icebox

instead of a dead body. I imagine this whole documentary based around plums

and nothing else. no dead bodies on ice, no conspiracies, no collar bombs.

just frozen plums, the glow of my television

trickling up into the moon's mouth,

you solving the mystery before the second act,

and tomorrow, if tomorrow decides to come.

[]

Ask me if the sky is as big today

as it was the last time we spoke,

when I jogged along the edge of Monterey Bay

hunting for a bloating gam of whales

to photograph for us

and dry heaved from withdrawal.

When our eyes and our mouths always took notes

for the poems we hadn't written yet.

Our throne, abdicated in the name of love,

or at least what a doctor convinced us was so.

Even after all those needling years,

I am still tenderly pulled apart

by the celluloid bloat of a face

turned miserably aglow with hormones.

Scammed, by the falsehood of medicinal reward.

In high school I wanted anything but a stomach

full of prescription disquiet. Just one cock

unexamined by labcoat strangers

and sperm born from my own cells.

Now in adulthood I only want to write poems

dedicated to Keith Charles

saying *no matter how we get a child, we'll both win*

to David Fisher on Six Feet Under,

because, given my own inconclusive fertility calculator

and my swimmers like butterfly teacups,

I say let's let those who glow just glow

and hope to someday make fire all the same.

There's a belly somewhere

now a living room painted by lamplight.

And if a set of intestines like tungsten,

then a set of breasts

mistaking the sky for the floor to match.

What gender is testosterone if not birdsong

singing *your sperm's in the gutter,*

your love's in the sink

against the gonadal potency of his own winded flute.

Yes, I am thick as a brick,

in that I can't peel backwards

and let the garden of suns spill from my ribs.

Yes, a decadence of light, as if everything I touch

knows how to breathe except myself.

I know you still sleep somewhere between the lips

you pressed against my cheek in a dormitory bedroom,

tonguing the sunset, patiently waiting for the wind.

Our running legs the color of sunburnt lemonade

have never stopped since we met.

I've been told the seven saddest words in the English

language are "he was going to be an acrobat,"

followed by "you need to see a fertility specialist."

Though, it is my humblest opinion that

all sentences I speak have already been cooked.

I could be the seventh son of the seventh son.

Everything I ever am will still require an incubator.

So perhaps I don't have it in me to love so hard.

Or perhaps I have never really loved anyone

quite as much as I have loved you.

O, to be swimming and swimming

until we cross paths again.

To never stop circling each other once we do.

FELINA

the mermaids in American water came just / after the A-bomb test in Nevada / Dad blamed Harding losing on the pharmaceutical dust / tornadoing around Mollenkopf Stadium / Mamaw sold my Lincoln Logs in the garage sale / said kids haven't played with Lincoln Logs since 'Nam / I saw David down the road waiting for our bus / and he waved at me with the laser pointer he stole off his dad / we played hangman with our breaths / looking like handwriting stuck in January air / that spring when The Melt came all the lunch ladies / started microwaving the soybean burgers instead / I stuffed a million suns into the pockets of my cargo pants / and stole 35-cent apple juice cartons / I ate a Cry Baby Sour Ice cup all alone in my mother's classroom / like I was fucking Steven Glansberg / you were in an art class somewhere halfway across the state / drawing pictures of all your beaches / the dealership said they put a moonroof in my Pontiac / so I could measure how far away God was / by ashing stars in the cupholder / and counting the mile-widths of toad-stranglers / yes we've seen thunder before / we just don't have a name for seeing it yet / can you believe we were all once ugly babies / hearing the This Charming Man riff for the first time / and thought, goodness I hope the lead singer doesn't ruin this for all of us / or that we played hooky just to see what happened / to Rafe and his evil twin on *Days of Our Lives* / or that the Bush administration / took the last traffic light off the highway / of course I miss / the suppers of buttered noodles and Coca-Cola / in front of a TV glowing *Man V. Food* reruns / turning the police scanner off just to hear How Deep Is Your Love / crawl out of Dad's living room stereo / and Dad saying Disco Demolition Night makes sense / in retrospect / or that one December when hometown garage band Acid / had their record go double-aluminum with no features / and there was snow falling in NYC on Christmas Eve / that looked like my mother in a hall of mirrors / back then our houses came from tin cylinders / with assembly required until the banks priced us out / and we couldn't afford an Uber / that would take us to the moon anymore / and the boys with Bill of Rights forearm tats / threw toilet cleaner bombs into yards /

and took baseball bats to mailboxes up the road / then there were the masculine street-fight lobotomies on SnapChat stories / I swear Chicken Fried blasting out of rusted Chevy S10 trucks / will be the death of me / all of this and the stink from falling steel plants / still disobeyed the wind and burnt down half the general store / all of this and the Ursuline cornerback still put a concussion / in Mario's head before Mario went and got drafted by the Giants / how romantic, the ways we've nuked each other to smithereens / just to come back pretty / the way the bar uptown closed every winter / and reopened under a new name / some say it was the hype / of the PlayStation 3 release that saved this city / for me, it was leaving and finding you

thank you to the following journals for publishing early versions of these poems (I apologize if the names and appearances have since changed): *HAD, Hobart, DEARPoetry, Big Lucks, Maudlin House, Sporklet, No Contact,* and *Glass: A Journal of Poetry.*

most of these poems were once a part of *The Neon Hollywood Cowboy* manuscript, but cut during different parts of the editing process. I'm grateful to give them their own space with this book.

"beyond the cowboys flushed in acid galloping" includes a quote from *The Road* by Cormac McCarthy.

"the freezing rain falling on the air conditioner" includes a lyric from "Jesus, Etc." by Wilco.

"I am on the phone with you / while watching *The Last Waltz* on a television" includes a lyric from "Helpless" by Neil Young.

"us: making love underneath the weight of an REO track" includes a quote from *Seinfeld.*

"tell me how all of my high school crushes are getting married" includes a lyric from "Bat Out of Hell" by Meat Loaf.

"I cannot sleep until I listen to" includes a lyric from "Radio Ga Ga" by Queen.

"you, suturing your swimming body" includes a lyric from "Transatlanticism" by Death Cab For Cutie.

"ask me if the sky is as big today" includes a lyric from "Thick as a Brick" by Jethro Tull and a quote from *Six Feet Under.*

thank you to word west for publishing this, my parents and friends for the support, Kaveh for the wonderful blurb, and Fleet Foxes for the title of this book.

Mark, the person on the cover of this book is James Dean.

Grown Ocean is for Alexia Austen, my Gran Torino.

Matt Mitchell is a poet and music critic in Columbus, Ohio.
He writes for Pitchfork, Bandcamp, CLASH, The Guardian, and elsewhere.
His debut poetry collection, *The Neon Hollywood Cowboy*, is out now from Big Lucks.
Follow him on Twitter @matt_mitchell48.

www.ingramcontent.com/pod-product-compliance
Lightning Source LLC
Chambersburg PA
CBHW020915080526
44589CB00011B/608